Look Who's Coming to Dinner!

by Mrs. Purifico's class
with Tony Stead

capstone

Imagine that you could invite anyone you wanted to dinner. Even more exciting, imagine that you could invite famous people from the present or the past. Our class thought about whom we might invite. Who's coming to dinner? Let's meet our guests!

YOU'RE
INVITED

Neymar da Silva Santos Junior

by Everett

Neymar da Silva Santos Jr. is a great soccer player. He is the captain of the Brazil national team. Neymar was born in Brazil in 1992. When he was 11, he joined FC Santos at the Brazil club to play soccer. When he was 18, he joined Brazil's national team.

In 2014 Neymar helped carry the Brazil Nation team to the quarterfinals of the World Cup. But in the final minutes against Colombia, Neymar got injured. Brazil still won the game but lost in the semifinals against Germany 7–1.

Neymar has won so many awards including Best Young Player in South America, the Golden Ball for best player, and many more.

This is why Neymar is the guest I'd want to have at my table. I'd like to know what it was like to train to be a great soccer player.

Zendaya

by Sumedha

I would really like for Zendaya to come to dinner. She is a model, singer, dancer, and actress. Plus, she gives back to the community.

Zendaya was born on September 1, 1996, in Oakland, California. Zendaya first came to fame in 2010 when she was in a show called *Shake It Up*. Early in 2013 Zendaya was cast on *Dancing with the Stars*. At the time, she was the show's youngest contestant at age 16. She placed runner-up. She also has a song called "Replay."

Zendaya is part of a group called Convoy of Hope, which helps people who are hungry. She also helps out with the Make-A-Wish Foundation, Keep a Child Alive organization, and the Children's Miracle Network.

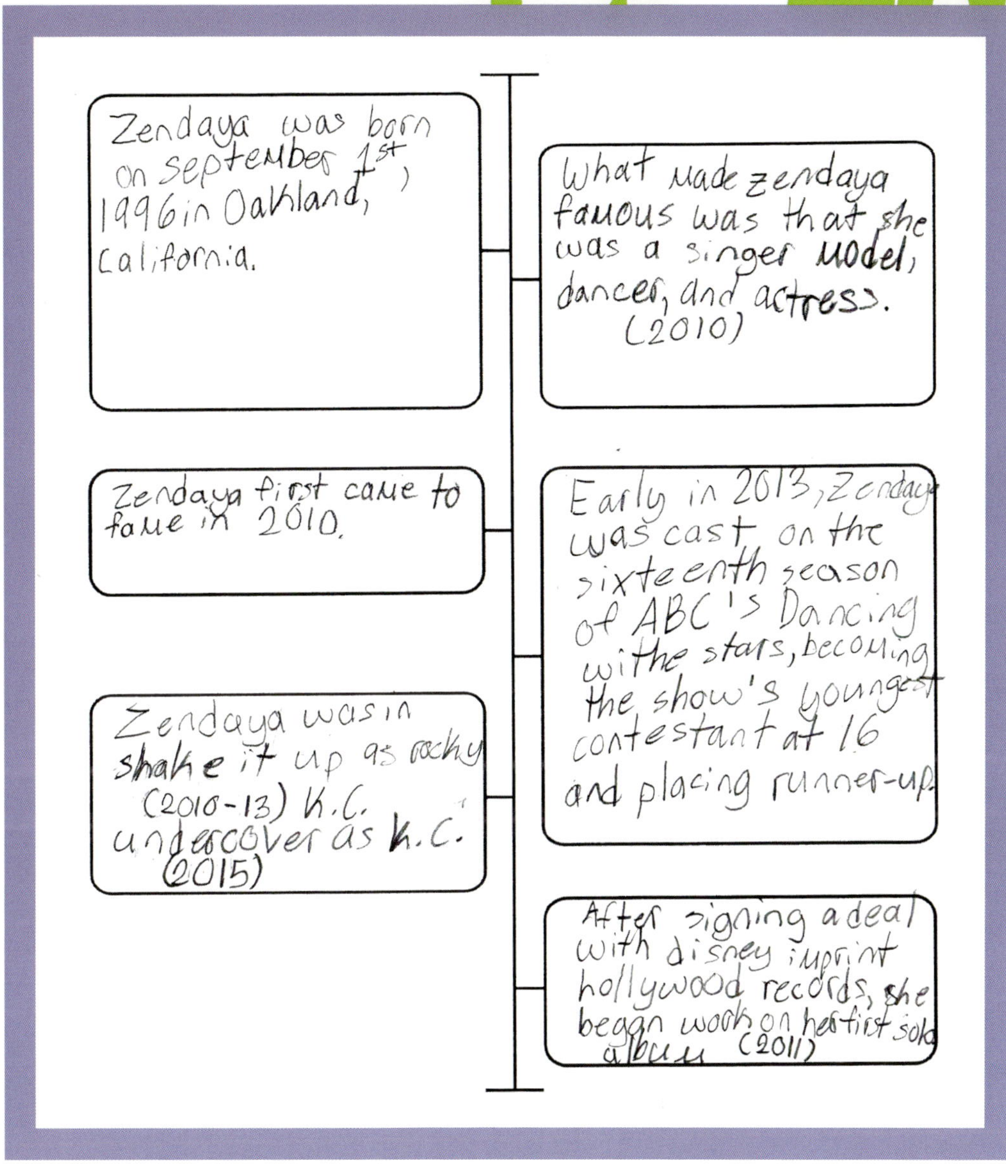

Zendaya is a positive person. She once said, "I try to be nice to everyone because I have no clue what's going on in their world." If I had dinner with her, I'd like to learn more about her.

Wilma Rudolph

by Makayla

I'd like Wilma Rudolph to come to dinner. She was the first African-American woman to win three gold medals at a single Olympics.

Here are some facts about Wilma Rudolph. First, when she was young, she had polio and had to wear a brace on her left leg. Her doctor said she would never walk again. But her mother said she would. Wilma believed her mom. Wilma did walk again with a lot of work.

Second, she played basketball in high school and Tennessee State University's track coach, Ed Temple, asked her to join his team. Third, in 1956 and 1960, Wilma qualified for the summer Olympics. Fourth, at the 1960 Olympics, Wilma won three gold medals and broke three world records.

Not only was Wilma one of the fastest women runners, she is an inspiration to me. I wish she were alive so that I could ask her questions about her life in person.

Henry Ford

by Nate

Henry Ford is famous for making the first mass-produced car on an assembly line. Henry Ford was born on July 30, 1863. He was one of eight children. During his young life, he liked to see how things worked. He loved to pull things apart and put them back together again.

As a young man, Henry Ford worked at Edison Illuminating Company to learn about electricity. He really liked vehicles, too. Henry made the Quadricycle on June 4, 1896. This was a horseless carriage. Then he started a company to build automobiles. And on October 1, 1908, Henry Ford built a car called the Model T. By 1927, 15 million Model Ts rode out of the Ford Motor Company, which Henry Ford owned.

Henry Ford died on April 7, 1947. If I met him at dinner, I would want to know what he'd like to invent today.

Marie Curie

by Gemma

Marie Curie is coming to dinner! Why would she be a good guest? Because she is famous for her work with X-rays and radioactivity. She also won the Nobel Prize twice.

Marie Curie was born in Poland in 1867. When she was 10, tragedy struck. Her mother got ill from tuberculosis and died. After her mother died, Marie and her sister Bronya struck a deal. Marie would work while Bronya went to school. Then Bronya would work while Marie studied. Marie wanted to go to the University of Warsaw, which only men attended. Instead, she went to Warsaw's "floating university." These were classes that were held in secret. In 1891 Marie became a student at the Sorbonne in France.

Marie
Curie

In 1894 Marie met Pierre Curie, a French physicist. She worked in his lab. They got married in 1895. She then took French physicist Henri Becquerel's work with uranium a little further. It was this work that caused her to make history. In 1903 she became the first woman to win the Nobel Prize in physics.

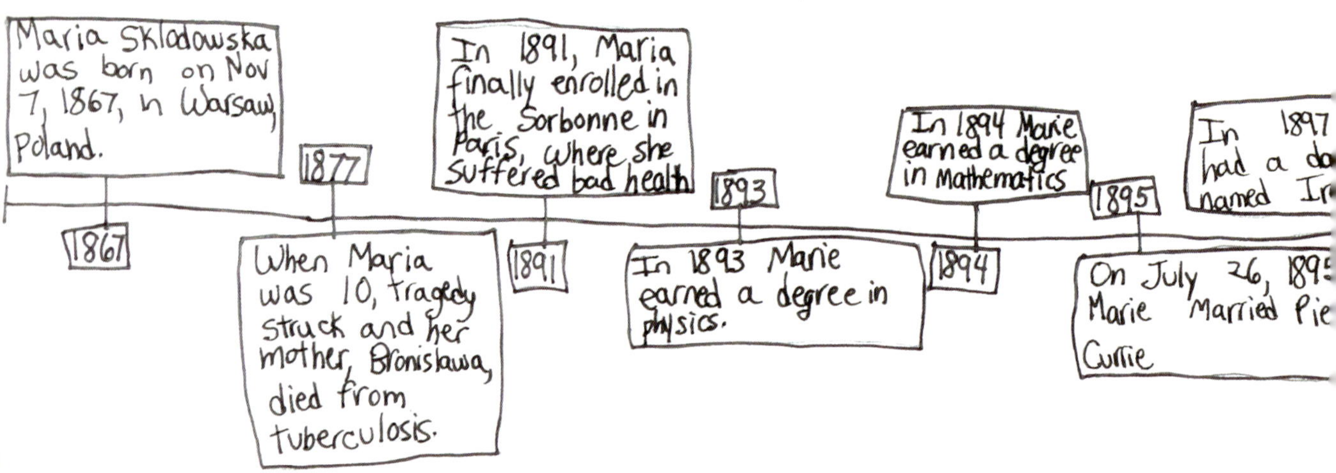

Eight years later, Curie received another great honor. She won a second Nobel Prize for her discovery of radium and polonium. She was the first scientist to win two Nobel Prizes!

Now you know what a determined scientist Marie Curie was and why she'd be an interesting dinner guest.

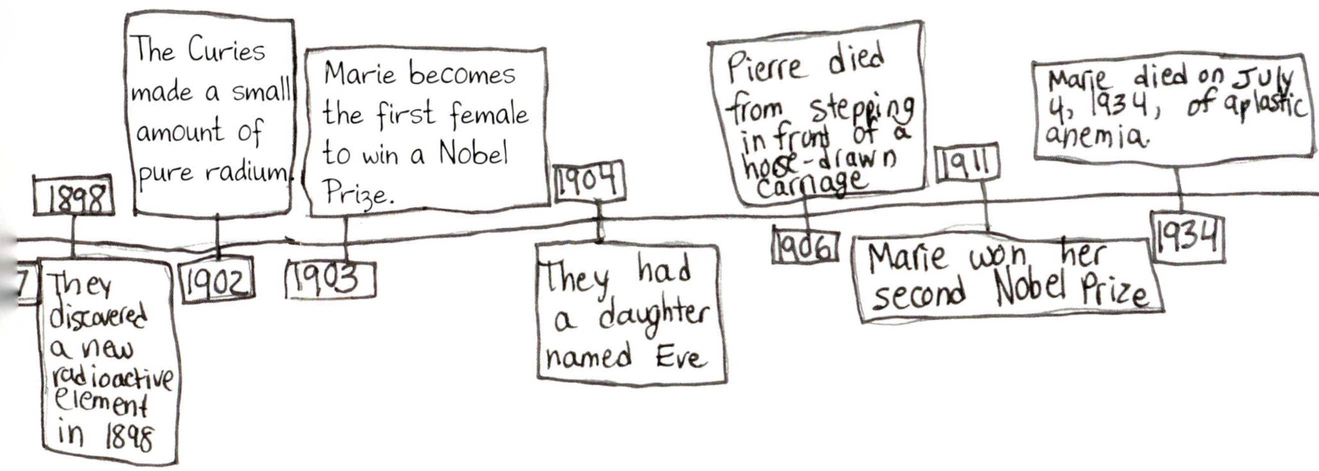

President Dwight D. Eisenhower

by Elishai

If you were to choose one president to have dinner with, whom would you choose? I would pick Dwight D. Eisenhower.

On October 14, 1890, Dwight Eisenhower was born in Texas. He had a lot of hobbies when he was younger, like playing baseball and football. Did you know he was also a cheerleader? In 1911 he got into West Point Military Academy. He graduated from West Point in 1915 and had lots of jobs in the military: second lieutenant, first lieutenant, major, and major general to name a few. During World War II, he led a famous invasion of Normandy called D-Day.

Dwight Eisenhower became president of the United States in 1953. He worked to bring peace to the world. President Eisenhower died in 1969.

If we had dinner together, I would like to know what his favorite job was. He would have a lot of history to share, too.

1890 born

1911 got into West Point Military Academy

1915 graduated from West Point; became second lieutenant

1916 promoted to first lieutenant

1920 promoted to major

1942 promoted to major general

1944 led the D-day invasion

1953 elected president

1969 died

Lionel Messi

by Gavin

Lionel Messi is famous for being one of the greatest soccer players of all time. He was born in Rosario, Argentina, on June 24, 1987. Messi was smaller than most of the kids his age. But when he was only 8 years old, he joined the youth system of Newell's Old Boys. This was a Rosario-based sports club. When he was 13, he began training with FC Barcelona's youth soccer club in Spain.

On May 1, 2005, Messi became the youngest player to score a goal for FC Barcelona. Since then, Messi has won lots of awards including World Player of the Year. That is why Messi is one of the greatest soccer players of all time and why I'd like to meet him.

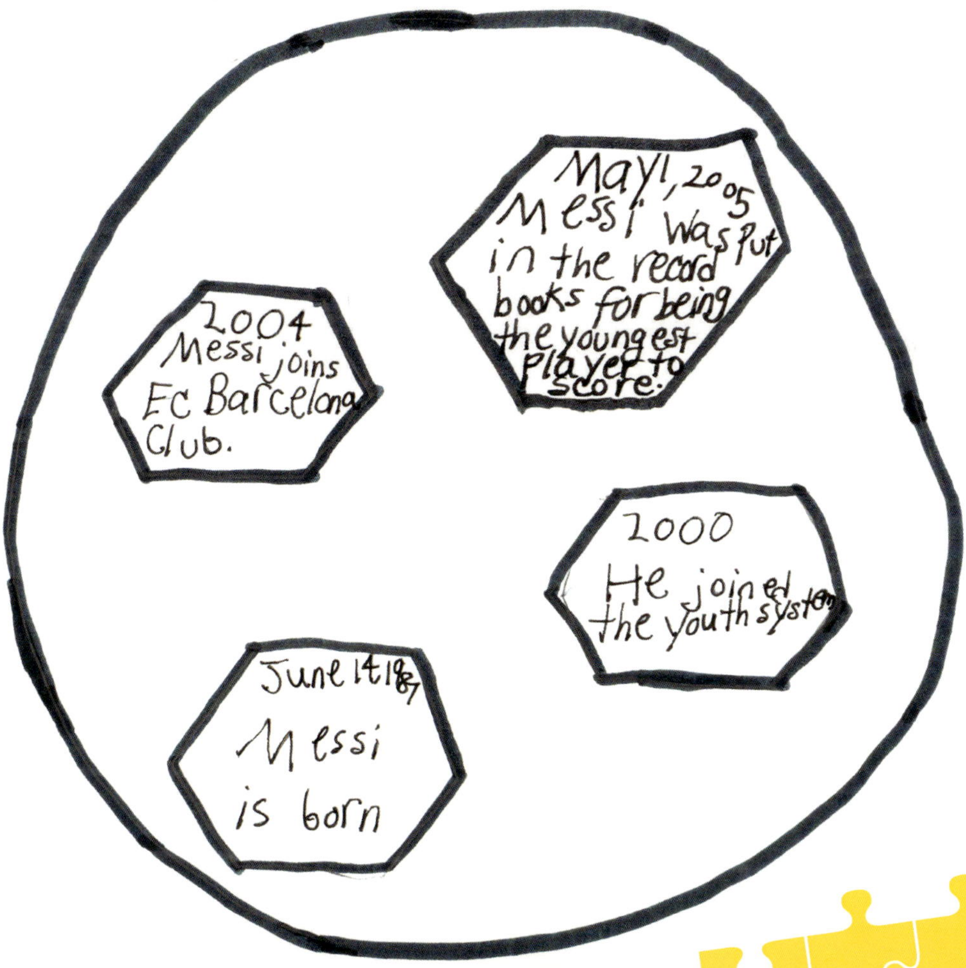

Adelle Adkins

by Lydia

Adele Adkins is coming to dinner! She was born in England on May 5, 1988. Her first album came out in 2008. It was called *19*.

When Adele was 21, she wrote the songs for her album *21*. The album included the songs, "Set Fire to the Rain," "Someone Like You," and "Rolling in the Deep." The album sold more than 30 million copies worldwide. Adele released an album called *25* in 2015. It has songs on there like "Hello." The songs on the album describe how she was feeling at age 25.

Adele has won lots of Grammy Awards in a short time. I'd like to meet her for dinner to find out what that was like.

GRAMMY

Joe Montana

by Alex

I want Joe Montana to come to dinner. He was born on June 11, 1956, in New Eagle, Pennsylvania. Joe grew up loving sports. In fact, he used to wait outside until his dad got home from work so they could throw around a football or baseball.

When Joe went to high school, he found a passion for football. Joe started college at Notre Dame in 1974 and played on their football team. But Joe was a seventh-string quarterback. That meant six other quarterbacks got to play before him.

Joe eventually took over as a starting quarterback. He led the team to the 1977 National Championship and the 1979 Cotton Bowl. As he said, “Always be prepared to start.”

After graduating from Notre Dame, Joe was selected by the San Francisco 49ers. He became their starting quarterback in his second season. During his career, Joe won his first Super Bowl against the Cincinnati Bengals in 1982. He also won the MVP (most valuable player) award. He then went on to win three more Super Bowls, which was a record-setting number.

Joe retired in 1995, after spending his last two years on the Kansas City Chiefs. It would be fun to hear about his many wins during dinner.

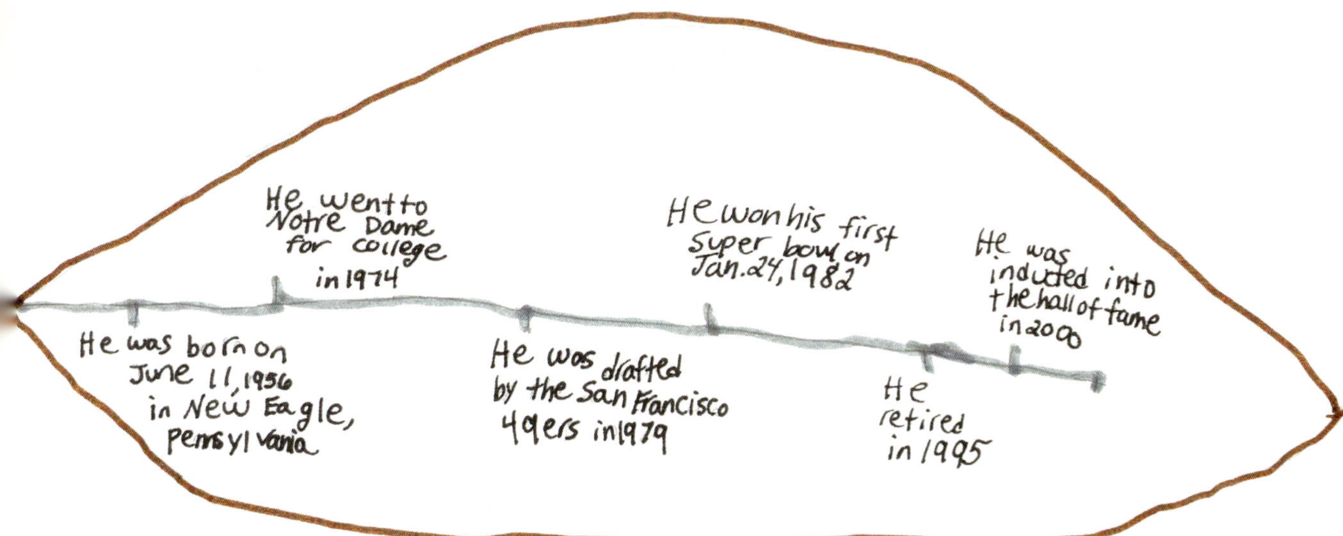

Our dinner guests include talented soccer players, a famous president, a groundbreaking scientist, popular singers, an Olympian, a most valuable player, and an inventor. Now imagine that you were having a dinner for famous people. Whom would you invite?